OPENING DAYS

OPENING DAYS

SPORTS POEMS

Selected by Lee Bennett Hopkins

Illustrated by Scott Medlock

Harcourt Brace & Company

San Diego   New York   London

Special thanks to Diane D'Andrade, Holly Yancy, and Lisa Peters
for the opportunity; Lee Bennett Hopkins for the wonderful inspiration;
Myrna Medlock, Steve Courchaine, Mitch Haddad, Kevin Parent,
Cara McGee, and Bonnie Phelps for their effort.

—S. M.

Compilation copyright © 1996 by Lee Bennett Hopkins
Illustrations copyright © 1996 by Scott Medlock

Library of Congress Cataloging-in-Publication Data
Opening days: sports poems/selected by Lee Bennett Hopkins;
illustrated by Scott Medlock.—1st ed.
p. cm.
Summary: A collection of eighteen poems about various sports
including baseball, skiing, karate, and tennis.
ISBN 0-15-200270-7
1. Sports—Juvenile poetry. 2. Children's poetry, American.
[1. Sports—Poetry. 2. American poetry—Collections.] I. Hopkins,
Lee Bennett. II. Medlock, Scott, ill.
PS595.S78063 1996
811.008'0355—dc20 94-43364

First edition
A B C D E
Printed in Singapore

OPENING DAYS

CONTENTS

KARATE KID

Jane Yolen

I am wind,
I am wall,
I am wave,
I rise, I fall.
I am crane
In lofty flight,
Training that
I need not fight.

I am tiger,
I am tree,
I am flower,
I am knee,
I am elbow,
I am hands
Taught to do
The heart's commands.

Not to bully,
Not to fight,
Dragon left
And leopard right.
Wind and wave,
Tree and flower,
Chop.
     Kick.
         Peace.
             Power.

THE SPEARTHROWER

Lillian Morrison

She walks alone
to the edge of the park
and throws into
the bullying dark
her javelin
of light,
her singing sign
her signed song
that the runner may run
far and long
her quick laps
on the curving track
that the sprinter surge
and the hurdler leap
that the vaulter soar,
clear the highest bar,
and the discus fly
as the great crowds cry
to their heroines
Come on!

ODE TO WEIGHT LIFTING

Gary Soto

Tony eats apples
On Saturday morning,
Two for each arm,
And one for the backs
Of his calves.
He's twelve
And a weight lifter in his garage.
He bites into an apple,
And, chewing,
He curls weights—
One, two, three . . .
His face reddens,
And a blue vein
Deepens on his neck—
Four, five, six . . .
Sweat inches down
His cheek. A curl of
Hair falls in his face—
Seven, eight, nine . . .
He grunts and strains—
Ten, eleven, twelve!

Tony curls his age,
And he would curl his weight
Of 83 pounds, but he
Would pull a muscle
In his arm.

Tony pulls off his T-shirt.
He flexes his biceps,
And apples show up in his arms.
"Pretty good," he says,
His fists clenched.
He takes another
Bite of apple,
And out of happiness
Bites the apples
In his biceps, tenderly
Of course. The teeth
Marks are pink,
His arms brown,
And his roar red as a lion's
With a paw swiping at air.

THE RUNNER

Walt Whitman

On a flat road runs the well-train'd runner,
He is lean and sinewy with muscular legs,
He is thinly clothed, he leans forward as he runs,
With lightly closed fists and arms partially rais'd.

I AM THE RUNNING GIRL

Arnold Adoff

i am the running girl

              there are walking girls

                 and jogging

      girls

                 in the streets

      girls who ride their

                      bikes

      and hike along brown

      country roads with

                    brothers

      and their friends

      and pull wild flowers

         for their hair

      but

i am the running girl

      there in the moving day

      and i cannot stop to

                    say

      hello

SPEED!

Monica Kulling

no hands
down the hill
no hands
just the wheel

brisk breeze
in my hair
such ease
not a care

my feet
steer the bike
my seat
sitting tight

wheels spin
this is speed!
wheels spin
all I need

THOUGHTS AFTER A FORTY MILE BIKE RIDE

Roy Wesson

My feet
And seat
Are beat.

THE SWIMMER

Constance Levy

The sun
underwater
makes chains of gold
that rearrange
as I reach through.
I feel at home
within this world
of sunlit water, cool and blue.
I sip the air;
I stroke;
I kick;
big bubbles bloom as I breathe out.
Although I have no tail or fin
I'm closer than I've ever been
to what fish feel
and think about.

FOUL SHOT   *Edwin A. Hoey*

With two 60's stuck on the scoreboard
And two seconds hanging on the clock,
The solemn boy in the center of eyes,
Squeezed by silence,
Seeks out the line with his feet,
Soothes his hands along his uniform,
Gently drums the ball against the floor,
Then measures the waiting net,
Raises the ball on his right hand,
Balances it with his left,
Calms it with fingertips,
Breathes,
Crouches,
Waits,
And then through a stretching of stillness,
Nudges it upward.

The ball
Slides up and out,
Lands,
Leans,
Wobbles,
Wavers,
Hesitates,
Exasperates,
Plays it coy
Until every face begs with unsounding screams—

And then
   And then
      And then,

Right before ROAR-UP,
Dives down and through.

TIES

Dabney Stuart

When I faded back to pass
Late in the game, as one
Who has been away some time
Fades back into memory,
My father who had been nodding
At home by the radio
Would wake asking
My mother, who had not
Been listening, "What's the score?"
And she would answer, "Tied."
While the pass I threw
Hung high in the brilliant air
Beneath the dark, like a star.

ICE SKATING

Sandra Liatsos

Higher and higher
I glide in the sky,
My feet flashing silver,
A star in each eye.
With wind at my back
I can float, I can soar.
The earth cannot hold me
In place anymore.

CHAIR LIFT

Maxine W. Kumin

Nobody holds your hand up there.
You sit alone in your moving chair.

It's not as smooth as an elevator.
It's scarier than an escalator.

Under your feet, the snowy humps
Of hills go by with jerks and bumps

And the only sound in the world is the clack
Of the chair lift clanking along its track.

The trees move past in a stiff parade
Like ice cream cones that giants made.

And suddenly, you're not a king.
You're not the head of anything.

Your feet are cold, your nose is runny,
Your stomach flutters and feels funny,

You wish the whole machine would stop
—And then, with a whir, you're off at the top.

SKIING

Bobbi Katz

Skiing is like being
part of a mountain.
On the early morning run
before the crowds begin,
my skis make
    little blizzards
as they plough
    through untouched powder
to leave fresh tracks
    in the blue-white snow.
My body bends and turns
    to catch each
bend and turn
    the mountain takes;
and I am the mountain
and the mountain is me.

TOMORROW!

Milton Bracker

Hoorah! hooray!
Be glad, be gay—
    The best of reasons
Is Opening Day.

And *cheering the players*
    And *counting the gate*
And *running the bases*
    And *touching the plate*.

And *tossing the ball out*
    And *yelling Play Ball!*
(Who cares about fall-out—
At least, until fall?)

Let nothing sour
This sweetest hour:
    The baseball season's
Back in flower!

BOYHOOD BASEBALL

Roger Granet

At bat, in bed, beneath the
sandlot sky, I would be
anyone I could imagine
in pinstripes, not pajamas.

At times it might be Mantle
knocking one deep into the Bronx
or Mays stealing third just a
second after Koufax strikes out the side.

And never noticing curfews,
only curveballs. I wait for one more
hanging knuckler, to hit one last homer,
to be a summer star far into the night.

SOCCER

Lee Bennett Hopkins

Twenty-two
prayers
on
reverent grass

kick
and
dribble
trap
and
pass—

sprint
and
run
tackle
and
fall—

all
for the
love
of the
sacred
ball.

LOVE FIFTEEN

Lillian Morrison

Swing to wallop,
stretch to smash
the bounding ball
O whip it down
and cover the ground
easily, lightly.

Smack the serve
and swift return,
stroke it fine,
drive it deep,
slam the lob's
looping flight,
Whang!

Here within
the chalked white
boundaries of
a sunny world,
test the best,
the body's wit
the body's reach
the body's might

Dancers in
a rigorous rite
who with every
ardent motion
praise the dark
and primal pulse
that pounds and bounces
in the light.

FINAL SCORE

Lee Bennett Hopkins

Eventually
there's
a final score
when
games
have ended

when
they're
over—

no more.

No more
    batting,
    kicking,
    tossing a ball—

No more
    stumbling,
    fumbling,
    rising up from a fall.

Games
have been played.

They're over.
           That's all.

Acknowledgments

Every effort has been made to trace the ownership of all copyrighted material and to secure the necessary permission to reprint these selections. In the event of any question arising as to the use of any material, the editor and the publisher, while expressing regret for any inadvertent error, will be happy to make the necessary corrections in future printings.

Grateful acknowledgment is made to the following for permission to reprint the material listed below:

Curtis Brown, Ltd., for "Final Score" and "Soccer" by Lee Bennett Hopkins, copyright © 1996 by Lee Bennett Hopkins; "Chair Lift" from *No One Writes a Letter to a Snail* by Maxine W. Kumin, copyright © 1962 by Maxine W. Kumin; "Karate Kid" by Jane Yolen, copyright © 1996 by Jane Yolen. All reprinted by permission of Curtis Brown, Ltd.

Harcourt Brace & Company for "Ode to Weight Lifting" from *Neighborhood Odes* by Gary Soto, copyright © 1992 by Gary Soto. Reprinted by permission of Harcourt Brace & Company.

HarperCollins Publishers for excerpt from *I Am the Running Girl* by Arnold Adoff, copyright © 1979 by Arnold Adoff. Reprinted by permission of HarperCollins Publishers.

Bobbi Katz for "Skiing," copyright © 1971. Reprinted by permission of the author, who controls all rights.

The New York Times Company for "Tomorrow!" by Milton Bracker, copyright © 1962 by The New York Times Company; "Boyhood Baseball" by Roger Granet, copyright © 1992 by The New York Times Company. Reprinted by permission.

Marian Reiner for "Speed!" by Monica Kulling, copyright © 1993 by Monica Kulling; "Ice Skating" by Sandra Liatsos, copyright © 1996 by Sandra Liatsos; "Love Fifteen" and "The Spearthrower" from *The Sidewalk Racer and Other Poems of Sports and Motion* by Lillian Morrison, copyright © 1968, 1977 by Lillian Morrison. All reprinted by permission of Marian Reiner for the authors.

Simon & Schuster, Inc., for "The Swimmer" from *A Tree Place and Other Poems* by Constance Levy, copyright © 1994 by Constance Kling Levy. Reprinted with permission of Margaret K. McElderry Books, an imprint of Simon & Schuster Children's Publishing Division.

Dabney Stuart for "Ties," which first appeared in *The Diving Bell* (Alfred A. Knopf, Inc., 1966). Reprinted by permission of the author, who controls all rights.

Weekly Reader Corporation for "Foul Shot" by Edwin A. Hoey. Special permission granted by *Read* magazine, published by Weekly Reader Corporation. Copyright © renewed 1989, 1962 by Weekly Reader Corporation.

Roy Wesson for "Thoughts after a Forty Mile Bike Ride," which originally appeared in *Language Arts,* National Council of Teachers of English. Copyright © 1982 by Roy Wesson.

The illustrations in this book were done in oil on paper.
The display type was set in Mantinia.
The text type was set in Granjon by Thompson Type, San Diego, California.
Color separations by Bright Arts, Ltd., Singapore
Printed and bound by Tien Wah Press, Singapore
This book was printed with soya-based inks on Leykam recycled paper,
which contains more than 20 percent postconsumer waste and has
a total recycled content of at least 50 percent.
Production supervision by Warren Wallerstein and Pascha Gerlinger
Designed by Lisa Peters

LS   811 OPE   OPE

Opening days : sports
poems.